T0197219

CREATE
MAGIC
AT
WORK

Practical Tools To Ignite
Human Connection

Amy Lynn Durham

BALBOA.PRESS
A DIVISION OF HAY HOUSE

Balboa Press books may be ordered through booksellers or by contacting:

Balboa Press
A Division of Hay House
1663 Liberty Drive
Bloomington, IN 47403
www.balboapress.com
844-682-1282

Because of the dynamic nature of the Internet, any web addresses or
links contained in this book may have changed since publication and
may no longer be valid. The views expressed in this work are solely those
of the author and do not necessarily reflect the views of the publisher,
and the publisher hereby disclaims any responsibility for them.

The author of this book does not dispense medical advice or prescribe
the use of any technique as a form of treatment for physical, emotional,
or medical problems without the advice of a physician, either directly
or indirectly. The intent of the author is only to offer information
of a general nature to help you in your quest for emotional and
spiritual well-being. In the event you use any of the information in
this book for yourself, which is your constitutional right, the author
and the publisher assume no responsibility for your actions.

Any people depicted in stock imagery provided by Getty Images are
models, and such images are being used for illustrative purposes only.
Certain stock imagery © Getty Images.

Print information available on the last page.

ISBN: 978-1-9822-6923-4 (sc)
ISBN: 978-1-9822-6924-1 (e)

Library of Congress Control Number: 2021910309

Balboa Press rev. date: 06/29/2021

TABLE OF
CONTENTS

PREFACE

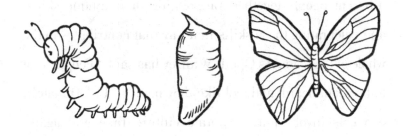

"What's your company's culture like?"

HOW MANY TIMES HAVE YOU BEEN ASKED THAT question? What is your answer? Do you even know? There are hundreds of books on the topic, yet many companies fail to truly distinguish themselves with an extraordinary company culture.

Your culture could be hard to define if you don't know where to start. I've seen executive after executive gather in meeting rooms and spend hours discussing what culture means to them, debating their visions. missions, and so on. Unfortunately, often none of the high-level consideration that goes into defining the culture ends up trickling down in any material way to the frontline employees, who are literally the faces and real cultures of your company.

Creating true company culture comes from bringing different people together, pinpointing their unique skills, and celebrating those skills in a way that contributes to the whole of the team. As Oprah Winfrey has said, "People want to be seen, heard, and feel like they matter." Unfortunately, ego gets involved in corporate culture time and again, especially at upper-management and executive levels, where some leaders feel they have to be in control or somehow demonstrate that they know more than everyone else. Letting go of that control and admitting you do not know everything can be a scary prospect for some. As a leader, you may feel deep down as though if you do let go or show that you actually don't know everything, your employees will think you're not worthy of the title or place that you hold within the organization. However, I've discovered that the exact opposite happens when a leader lets go of that control. For example, some of the most powerful statements I've made as a leader have been:

I MADE A MISTAKE.

WHAT ARE YOUR THOUGHTS ON THIS?

I'M NOT AN EXPERT ON THIS TOPIC.

LET'S CALL BECKY AND GET HER FEEDBACK.

WE HAVE A PROBLEM THAT NEEDS TO BE
SOLVED, AND I DON'T HAVE ALL THE ANSWERS.
I'D LIKE EACH INDIVIDUAL TO BRING TWO
PROPOSED SOLUTIONS TO OUR MEETING.

Lack of trust is another stumbling block for building a real-life, amazing company culture. This issue can present itself in many ways within an organization, such as an executive who thinks they know better than the masses and micromanages the employees instead of granting them real responsibilities and decision-making powers. Or fear-based management based on the flawed idea that employees won't be as productive because they aren't worried about keeping their jobs or striving for more profit at all times. There are still thousands of companies that use distorted, negative, competitive tactics to pit employees against each other in order to reach their goals. While these companies may have earned the profits or revenue they were striving for at that particular time, what about all the hidden costs? Were the employees burned out, driving them to leave the company and resulting in large costs of rehiring and retraining? Was mental stress carried into employees' home lives, leading to employees with increased health problems? Was so much animosity created between people that they can no longer collaborate harmoniously?

Think of the alternative. Could the profits have been even higher if there had been healthy competition, where everyone contributes to the overall goal and plays a part in its success?

Do you want to be known as a stress reliever or a stress inducer?

Many business leaders are "all about the numbers," watching results on revenue streams constantly. However, they ignore the data that clearly shows that building a positive company culture through autonomy, flexibility, and effectively using people's talents and skills actually increases profitability. This is what I like to call the "selectively data-driven executive." In a time when people no longer work at one particular company for their entire lives and instead job-hop around, the cost of attrition has a real impact on a company's bottom line.

It is worthwhile to let go of that fear of loss of control or fear that people won't do the right things. If you invest in employees' emotional well-being, helping to foster more human connection and elevating emotional intelligence (EQ) and spiritual intelligence (SQ), you will attract the individuals to your organization who are willing to go above and beyond. They will do this because you chose to give them the tools they need to become better leaders and better people.

Surrounding yourself with unique, talented individuals is the first key to cracking the code in building a phenomenal company culture. And guess what? You are already surrounded with unique, talented individuals most of the time. It just takes getting to know them on a more personal level, realizing what their strengths are, and developing those strengths for the benefit of the whole team or company. This handbook is designed to give you practical tools that you can utilize to bring out the unique qualities of your employees and build a truly positive company culture that you are excited about and proud of. These practical tools are also great exercises and modalities that you can utilize during one-on-one sessions with employees or clients if you are an executive or life coach.

SOME GROUND RULES TO PONDER

NEVER SCHEDULE A TEAM-BUILDING EXERCISE or a meeting centered on increasing employee engagement or morale during people's regular time off work. When you do this, it says to the employee, "We care about you but not enough to take away your time when we need you working hard for what we pay you." And to make matters worse, you are taking time away from their personal lives. Respect for personal lives and time will gain your employees' loyalty in the long term. When you carve out time during regular business hours to conduct personal growth and development, you are sending a strong message that this is an important part of a thriving business.

People will forget what you said. People will forget what you did. But people will never forget how you made them feel."
—MAYA ANGELOU

Utilizing the following activities will not only make a positive impact on your bottom line but will also send ripple effects out into the world because of the progressive differences you make in people's lives. Each of the following exercises and modalities can be incorporated during your regularly scheduled, in-person meetings, and many can be done virtually. Some methods can be scheduled strictly for the team build without any regular business items being discussed. If you do use these activities during normal meeting times, I recommend first covering essential business information and initiatives that need to be addressed, and then ending the sessions with a team-build exercise. This way, employees leave with a feeling of positivity and beneficial self-development techniques to make them better leaders when they return to their respective employees. More often than not, they will do a similar team-building exercise with their employees who report to them, and you have created a nice ripple effect in your organization.

Incorporating these techniques into one-on-one meetings with your employees or clients as modalities is a helpful way to facilitate thinking and connecting with each other. This practical guide of real-world items and exercises/modalities will move you from the thinking-and-talking-about-company-culture phase to the action phase. Let's act!

Action has magic, grace
and power in it.
—JULIA CAMERON

JOURNALING TOGETHER AND WITH A *TWIST*

Every morning we are born again.

What we do today is what matters most.

—BUDDHA

ONE OF THE MANY HEALTH BENEFITS OF journaling is its ability to alleviate stress. Working to reduce the stress levels of your employees aids in quieting their left brains, the analytical side, and opening space for their right brains to engage in creativity and inspiration. This is when the true magic happens! You are opening space for them to build skill sets that cannot be replaced by a computer.

You will be amazed by the gratitude and loyalty your employees will display when you set aside company time to work on personal well-being. Nothing demonstrates caring more than when a leader invests their company's time in employees' personal growth. Journaling is an extremely beneficial team-building tactic to use with men—as are all of the exercises included here—because many boys are taught to suppress their intuition and creativity. Giving those same boys, who are now men, a safe space to express what has been suppressed will aid in emotional balance and help them become better leaders and better men.

If you have some trepidation about trying this exercise with a group of boiler-room mentality individuals who may think journaling is for the sixteen-year-old girl writing in her diary, start the exercise by citing all the benefits that they will receive by journaling. Who can argue with you when you are offering time to do something that "reduces stress," "improves immune function," "keeps memory sharp," "boosts mood," and "strengthens emotional functions," as Kasee Bailey noted in her blog entry, "5 Powerful Health Benefits of Journaling."

Here's how to get started.

1. Set time aside at the end of your meeting for your team to spend in quiet reflection journaling. There are a variety of journal prompt cards available online; I've created a deck of journal prompt cards specifically designed for the workplace as a companion for this exercise that you can find on the Create Magic At Work website. They all give specific topics and questions to help inspire journaling. If you have the budget, make the exercise more meaningful by buying each member of your team a journal and pen to use just for this purpose, and hand them out as gifts before you begin. If you have a team name or logo, you might even want to have journals printed with that on the cover.

2. To begin, take out your journal prompt cards and place them facedown. Go around the room and have each person draw a card. Make sure to stress that whatever card they choose, its message is specifically meant for them.

3. Give everyone about fifteen minutes of silence to reflect on the topic of the card that they chose

and then write about it in their journals. During that time, you can play some peaceful, meditative music.

4. Once everyone is finished, open the floor for discussion. Ask for volunteers to share with the group what their topic was and what they wrote in their journals. It is imperative that you do not require everyone to share. Just create a safe space where everyone is offered a chance to have a voice within the group. All teams have certain personality dynamics, and some individuals tend to be more talkative and outspoken compared to others. Always make it a point to recognize the quiet individuals, and ask them if they would like to share. But give them respect and reverence if they choose to keep their journaling moment to themselves and opt out of sharing. If you call on someone who is traditionally very quiet and they say they do not want to share, simply say, "No problem. I just wanted to make sure you had a voice and were heard by the group if you wanted the opportunity." Then move on to the next person.

5. End the session when everyone who wants to share has done so. I always let everyone keep the journal prompt card they chose as a memento from the experience.

DARE TO DREAM EXERCISE

The Grass is Greener Right Here.

—DAVID AULT

IF YOU ARE LOOKING TO INCORPORATE A VERSATILE, creative activity into one of your group meetings or individually with a client (virtual or in person), this exercise is a perfect choice. You can facilitate it for fifteen minutes or up to an hour, depending on the number of participants and the amount of sharing you allow. Just the act of visualizing the removal of the perception of what we "have to do" and replacing it with choices results in a huge stress reduction and cultivates feelings of empowerment. Giving employees permission to work on their personal goals while at work builds loyalty and returns on this time investment will last a lifetime.

1. Before beginning this exercise, have every participant shut down all their electronics so there are no distractions. Dim or turn off the lights in the room. I like to use essential oils in this exercise (as well as in many other exercises). Offer each individual a drop of lavender or a good balancing essential oil in their hands. There are so many to choose from. I've included some recommendations on the "Resources" page at the end of the book.

2. Ask the participant(s) to close their eyes so that they can more easily calm down and get grounded. (Of course if anyone feels uncomfortable doing that, it's not required.) Instruct everyone to rub their hands together to activate the oils, and then hold their hands in front of their faces, inhaling deeply three times.

3. Ask everyone to imagine their life if they never had to work again or earn a paycheck. Here are a few questions you might ask to help them consider this idea more effectively: What would your life look like? What would you do with the rest of your life? What happens when you release the belief that you have to wake up and earn a paycheck every day to get by? Imagine you have everything you need financially ... now what?

   Spend about three minutes in silence, letting them visualize what life would look like under these circumstances.

4. Restore the lights. Ask the participant(s) to open their eyes, and hand them a blank piece of paper and a pen. For the next five to ten minutes, have each individual write down a list of five things they would do if they never had to work a day in their life again.

5. When everyone is finished with compiling their lists, open the group for sharing and discussion. Remember, not everyone is required to share, but everyone is welcome to and will always have

a voice if they need to use it. You are just offering psychological safety to share.

6. Now for the punch line. As the leader or coach, at the end of the meeting you are going to require each individual to pick at least two items on the list that they are committing to accomplishing right now or within a certain time frame. The reality is most people do have to get up and go to work every day to earn a paycheck. But the reality, also, is if you prioritize your time and goals appropriately, you can accomplish many things that you may think you can't accomplish because you are telling yourself, *I have to work.*

In the past when I've moderated this exercise, I have had some really serious, as well as humorous, goals achieved. For example, I saw one person note that they would like to travel to Europe, and the goal was achieved by that summer. I've seen participants write down fitness and health goals; fitness is often something that people who work long hours must sacrifice. But if you can inspire others to dedicate time to their health and wellness, it will pay you back hundreds of times over in sound decision-making and positive leadership, not to mention the savings in health costs and losses to the business if, or when, they have to take leave for medical or stress issues. Another employee in this exercise said he wanted to lie on the couch all day and smoke meats in a meat smoker, which gave everyone a good laugh. Fast-forward to this employee's birthday, and the team pitched in money and gifted him with a meat smoker. He was extremely touched. It made something fun and humorous impactful and built camaraderie within the group at the same time. Now, after the exercise, the laughs, and the gift, if an individual on the team needed some extra help, our meat-smoker employee would be more willing to take their call and work together rather than just fend for himself, once again contributing to the collective success of the company and team.

Remember to have your employees set deadlines for when they would like to accomplish these, "if I never had to work," goals and mark them on their calendars. Follow up in casual conversations with each individual to see how their progress has been. Do not follow up with them as you would for a work task or project. This should not become a stressful task that they have to accomplish.

Revisit this exercise in another six months to a year to help with changing priorities and life events.

INTENTION-
SETTING
EXERCISE

*Intention leads to behaviors which lead to habits which
lead to personality development which leads to destiny.*
—JACK KORNFIELD

HELPING A GROUP OR INDIVIDUAL SET INTENTIONS
for what they want to bring into their lives, or possibly let go
of in their lives, is a very powerful practice. Many times we
can get extremely caught up in our day-to-day routines, and

we forget to stop, take a step back, and look at ourselves, our businesses, and our long-term or even short-term goals with an aerial view. This exercise gives people time to reflect and ask themselves, *What do I really want in my life? What do I want to let go of that is no longer serving me?*

This exercise gives your employees permission to take the time to do this. The tool that I like to use with intention-setting exercises is flying wish paper. If you've never heard of it, it is awesome! (I've highlighted my favorite types on the "Resources" page.) You can also just use journals or sheets of paper for this exercise, but I highly recommend the flying wish paper for the *wow* effect.

If you are able to meet with your team in person, this is a great exercise to gather everyone around after a meeting or after dinner. I once rented out a bed and breakfast for my team, and we did this intention-setting exercise before everyone went to bed. It was extremely impactful. This will connect your team with each other on a higher level, build psychological safety, and bond everyone together by building empathy and respect for each other.

Hand out a piece of wish paper to every individual and ask them to write two to three intentions, wishes, or goals that they would like to bring into their life. Stress to the group that this is their own personal-growth exercise, and the intentions can be either business-related or personal. Once they write their intentions on the wish paper, ask for volunteers to share their intentions. If it is a smaller group, then everyone should have a chance to share.

Saying these intentions aloud in front of their peers has a powerful effect and helps to bring those intentions into their lives. Be sure to keep an eye on the silent ones in the group. Call on them and ask if they would like to share. But if they opt not to share with the group, respect their space. I've discovered that by doing this you are letting people know that they are seen and can be heard if they choose to be. Make sure not to underestimate the quiet individuals in a group. Some of them are the most deeply impacted by these exercises. I've had many individuals who are more comfortable in a one-on-one setting pull me aside to let me know how inspiring this was and thanked me for the session.

Once everyone has had an opportunity to share, if you are using the wish paper, ask everyone to crinkle up their paper, roll it into a vertical tube, set it on a little square of cardboard, and light the tip on fire. Everyone can light their wish paper on fire at once, or you can choose to go around the room and have each person share and light theirs one by one. The intentions that were shared burn to the bottom of the board, lift off the board, and fly into the air, sending their intentions off into the universe. It is a very magical thing to witness. People love the feeling of watching and being a part of this.

If you want to delve even deeper with your intention-setting exercises, you can time them with the phases of the moon. The new moon is a great time to set intentions for things that you would like to bring into your life. You can share with everyone that as the moon grows, you can watch your intentions grow. In addition, if you are near the time of a full moon, it is a great time to let go of something that is not serving you in your life.

If you don't care about the moon phases one way or another, have your team pick either something to let go of or something they want to bring into their life and write it on the paper. Either way, the *wow* effect and impact will be there.

Be prepared to respect whatever may be shared. As a leader or coach, many people look to you as a mentor and someone to look up to. Therefore, things may be shared that are very sacred or personal. I recommend just holding space for that moment in time and then moving on afterward. For example, I performed the flying wish paper exercise with a team around the time of the full moon, and I recommended writing two to three items down that you want to let go of or release in your life. One individual shared with the group that he was going to forgive his parents. He took a deep breath, lit the paper on fire, and we all watched it burn and fly into the air. It was a beautiful moment. Others may share something humorous, such as releasing their anger that their favorite team didn't win in the NBA finals.

Either way, lead the exercise with no judgment, and let everyone share what they wish. The different personalities and the acceptance of where each individual is in their life are what make the world less boring and more fun to partake in.

You can also use this exercise in front of larger crowds, and it has a very profound impact. I once helped the CEO of a large organization let go of a really rough prior year for the company in front of all his executive leaders. It was extremely cathartic for him simply to write the prior year's number down on wish paper in front of everyone, light the wish paper on fire, watch it burn down and then fly up in the air, and finally, let it all go and move forward to what came next. It was not only healing for himself but for his team who watched him do it. I was honored to be a part of it.

MORE
THAN
S'MORES

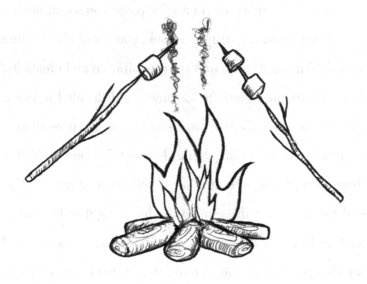

You can't stop the waves, but you can learn to surf.

—JON KABAT-ZINN

AS I WAS IN THE PROCESS OF WRITING THIS BOOK,
I reached out to my former team of eight district managers and
asked each of them what their favorite team-building activity
had been when we worked together. The overwhelming

winner was when I coordinated a meeting and then a team-building activity at the beach. I had initially hesitated to include this activity in this book because it felt so simple. But because of the tremendous feedback they shared, I just couldn't leave it out.

Recently I saw a piece of advice posted on social media. It said that if you are writing a book, you should be reading a lot so that you can tap into your inspiration and creativity. I was sitting on a plane to Colorado and decided to crack open Brené Brown's *Dare to Lead*. I had been reading it while I was at my prior job and had not finished it. At this time, I had been on hiatus for a little over three months, and for those first three months, the thought of looking at another leadership book was not appealing to me at all. I was detoxing and taking a break. But on that flight, I opened the book again, and *bam!* Right there in the middle of the book, the universe gave me the answer as to why this very simple team build had been so impactful to my crew. She referenced an article in the *Harvard Business Review* that was about companies that reported high levels of exhaustion. A research team had examined what was driving high levels of exhaustion, and they discovered that the employees were not exhausted from their workloads per se but because they were lonely. The loneliness was causing the exhaustion. I immediately searched for the article and found it: "America's Loneliest Workers, According to Research." I was excited when I saw that one of the contributing authors of the article was Shawn Achor, author of *The Happiness Project*.

I had a light bulb moment on the plane. *This is why!* I realized. This is why my employees felt our beach bonfire was so impactful to them. Because they were exhausted and felt lonely. It was an exercise that brought all of them together in one space and caused them to view each other with empathy and not just as a coworker they have to put up with, compete with, or for that matter, step over on their way to the top. The research from the article showed that "loneliness threatens not only our physical health and well-being, but also our livelihood." It also provided evidence that loneliness has the same effect as fifteen cigarettes a day in terms of health care outcomes and health care costs. Yet we are often blind to this hidden drain on health and revenue. "Lonelier workers perform more poorly, quit more often, and feel less satisfied with their jobs—costing employers upwards of $3.5 billion in the U.S. alone." It was discovered that one of the biggest amplifiers to help alleviate loneliness was for leaders to assist individuals in having shared meaning and collective wins in a supportive work environment. The article also made sure to counsel leaders to look for signs of loneliness such as social withdrawal and diminished mood.

I had called this meeting and required everyone to attend in person because I recognized that my team needed some fun and a break. I booked a hotel on the beach in Monterey, California, and offered the ocean-view rooms to the top performers of the week so they had something to look forward to.

Here is how you can replicate the "S'mores and More Beach Bonfire":

If you have the budget, have the hotel set it up for you. We had a firepit, tiki torches, and an entire bar cart full of drinks and s'more kits ready for us.

On another occasion, I purchased all the materials myself, and we had a lot of fun setting up the scene together. After our meeting, I took everyone to a nice dinner to ensure they were well fed so no one was "hangry." Then everyone gathered at the beach for roasting s'mores and enjoying camaraderie around the firepit. And OK, maybe there was a cocktail or two that was consumed!

Here is the most important part of this activity: I

required that each individual bring their favorite quote or inspirational message to share with the group around the fire. I kicked off the event by reading a motivational passage about the ocean. Then we went around to each individual who had brought their favorite inspirational message, and they had an opportunity to share it and talk about the reason it was so impactful to them. The fact that each person was able to share what meant most to them and why with several active listeners is the reason this worked toward alleviating their loneliness. Each person felt seen and heard for during that time at the beach, they felt as if they mattered. It was an amazing experience and one that I will never forget. And clearly, my team has never forgotten either.

If you aren't near a beach, you could do the same exercise with a firepit at someone's home or at a campsite or park. Just make sure that you get everyone together in person, if you can, and have them participate in this shared bonding experience. If you are a leader of many individuals and are geographically challenged, I encourage you to try this in a virtual, dedicated team meeting over the phone or through video conference. It will still be impactful by helping to reduce that loneliness factor. The deep connection and openness that occurs by just offering the space to share will be dramatically impactful to all involved.

I like to think of this team build as one of those amazing recipes that chefs cook in which there are only a few simple ingredients, and yet it tastes phenomenal! You will never forget the meal because it was so uncomplicated and cooked to perfection.

SHADOW
WORK

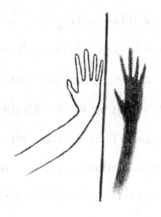

*Unless we do conscious work on it, the shadow
is almost always projected: that is, it is neatly
laid on someone or something else so we do
not have to take responsibility for it.*

—ROBERT JOHNSON

AS LEADERS IN THE WORKPLACE, ONE OF THE
most important things we must do is focus on our own
personal growth. We must make sure that we don't fall
into the trap of pointing the finger toward everyone else to
grow and then neglect or ignore our own growth. The most

effective leaders and lifelong learners are always looking for ways to improve themselves in order to serve others. Therefore, shadow work is so important.

Shadow work is the process of diving into the unconscious aspects of our personalities and exploring why we have shoved those aspects down into the shadows. It is not good or bad. Light and dark simply exist, and we must acknowledge both to grow and heal. When we work with the shadow parts of ourselves it allows us to help alleviate negative effects in our lives. By focusing on healing ourselves instead of focusing on how others need to change, we shift the overall healing of collective humanity forward much faster. In Jungian psychology, the shadow—also known as id, shadow aspect, or shadow archetype—is either an unconscious aspect of the personality that the conscious ego does not identify in itself or the entirety of the unconscious, that is, everything of which a person is not fully conscious. Following, I offer different themes that ask reflective questions for you to journal. Write the answers to the questions, and spend some time as a leader doing your own inner work. You can also use these topics in group discussions or one-on-one work with a client. Many of these reflective questions can be used in your "question bank" as an executive coach or leader when helping a client or employee.

I am proud of my unique gifts, and I am
excited to share them with others.

Creativity: This shadow-work theme surrounds creation, confidence, abundance, and self-expression.

- What parts of myself have I hidden from the workplace?
- Where have I had an unsupportive attitude?
- Where have I acted in a way that does not match my moral standards or beliefs?

I make decisions for others the way I
would want them made for me.

Justice: This shadow-work theme surrounds equality, balance, and karma.

- Is my self-talk positive, loving, and encouraging?
- Have I judged myself too harshly?
- Where have I acted in a way that does not match my moral standards or beliefs?
- What can I do to ensure that I speak about my coworkers in an empathetic, nonjudgmental way?

The words I speak create my world.

Magic: This shadow-work theme surrounds our abilities to take action in order to create magic in our lives.

- What part of me is attracted to chaos?
- What do I want to create this week with the words that I speak?
- Where have I been overly self-promoting to create a false sense of personal power?

I gift myself moments of solitude and retreat in order to be in harmony. (Amy Lynn Durham)

Meditation: This shadow-work theme surrounds meditation, retreat, and being in harmony with yourself before you attempt to be in harmony with the world.

- Am I holding onto something that I need to release in my life?
- What decisions can I make today or this week that will give me peace of mind within the next month?
- Is there an issue in my life that I need to make a decision about in order to move forward?

I am open to adventure, and I leave space for
the unimaginable to appear in my life.

Courage: This shadow-work theme surrounds courage, adventure, and being passionate about your personal and work lives.

- Am I envisioning my future so rigidly that I am not allowing for the abundant unimaginable to appear?
- Am I self-sabotaging by setting the bar too high for myself with regard to my short-term goals?
- What parts of my life have I closed off and have been afraid to try something new?

I stay flexible & persistent when working through
problems, knowing the only way out is through.

Flexible Persistence: This shadow-work theme surrounds persistence, overcoming obstacles, and seeing solutions for problems that you may have been missing.

- What problems at work have I been avoiding that I need to actively work through?
- What solutions have I been missing that could be available to me? (Try rapid writing five options.)

I make time to daydream and let ideas

take shape into my reality.

Be Inventive: This shadow-work theme surrounds our inner mad scientists, artists, and virtuosos.

- What can I do to have a more open mind?
- What do I feel about myself? How can I love myself more?

I celebrate the success of others, knowing

there is plenty for us all.

– LOUISE HAY

Altruism: If you are a leader in the workplace, you are often in a position to be altruistic and charitable. This shadow-work theme involves digging deep within ourselves to see if we have been giving from a place of compassion or from a place of ego in order to feel dominant over others.

- Do I perform random acts of kindness to validate that I am a good person to myself?
- What are the feelings I have when I am charitable? Are they feelings of understanding or superiority?

I take time to reward myself for the work that I accomplish.

Renewal: This shadow-work theme involves digging deep within ourselves to see if we have been refusing to change habits that may keep us stuck.

- Where have I been caught up in looking for the approval of others?
- What places in my life feel stuck, and what choices can I make to help myself move forward?
- What beliefs do I hold that may be too rigid, not allowing for new opportunities to unfold?

*I embrace change and give up the need
to know what happens next.*

Transformation: This shadow-work theme surrounds transformation, embracing endings, and releasing the old to welcome new beginnings.

- What areas in my work have I been too aggressive or pushy?
- What parts of my life have I been fighting to control?
- What can I do to approach life in a peaceful way?

MISCELLANEOUS MODALITIES/ TEAM-BUILDING ACTIVITY IDEAS

Pay attention to what has heart and meaning.

—*THE FOUR-FOLD WAY,* ANGELES ARRIEN

MAKE TIME FOR TEA

Drinking tea is such a beautiful ritual that connects humans with each other and is practiced in many cultures all over the world. For one hour (or whatever length of time works for you), gather your team and just sit, drink tea, and be. It is nice if everyone is drinking the same kind of tea from the same pot. No cell phones, no music. Just focus on the slow drinking of the tea and connecting with each other.

You can add to this exercise by setting up the space with pillows or blankets for each individual to sit on. Scattered candles or plants will add to the ambience. You might want to start the session by passing a burning palo santo or sage stick around and asking each individual to set a positive intention for what they would like to bring into their lives as they ingest their tea with the group.

Provide teacups with unique symbols or quotes on them. As you drink the tea, ask each person to describe the cup they chose and to reflect on why they chose that one. You can also use prompt cards or coaching questions. Have each person draw a question from the deck and reflect on the answer with the group. (I've highlighted sources for my favorite types on the "Resources" page.)

Make it special. Make the time and stop scrolling and running off to the next task for just a while. *Sidenote:* This could be done as a wine-tasting team-building activity as well.

RESTORATIVE YOGA SESSIONS

Have a trained yoga instructor do a private session for you and your team. If you do a restorative session, it is very low impact, so almost everyone will be able to participate without any risk of injury. This can be done by most yoga instructors at a very reasonable price and coordinated for an hour. At the end have the instructor lead a guided visualization on sending positive energy to people in the world. If they have sound healing bowls, this is a great time to incorporate that stress-reducing technique into this practice.

QUICK WAYS TO MAKE AN IMPACT

You never know when a moment and a few
sincere words can have an impact on a life.

—ZIG ZIGLAR

CREATE APPRECIATION ANCHORS

A huge part of emotional intelligence is having an emotional management strategy. One of the ways to help facilitate this is to have an appreciation anchor. According to the Institute for Health and Human Potential, the brain cannot experience fear and appreciation at the same time. Appreciation releases counter chemistry that increases perspective, energy, and complex thought. An appreciation anchor pushes back on our negativity biases.

In the past, I have created appreciation anchors for many events with employees and teams. Crystal pouches are one of my favorites. I typically consult with a crystal master for the best combination to create the energy and feeling I am trying to bring into the meeting, conference, or space. For example, for one national conference I created a positivity pouch that contained smoky quartz, amethyst, yellow citrine, and pyrite. This combination was meant to help keep people grounded, guard against negativity, and increase productivity. I put the crystals in tiny pouches with little labels and handed them out at the conference. People love receiving positive anchors like that. I also use crystals as anchors for leaders/coaches when they have a public-speaking engagement. Anytime someone has to present in front of an audience, it is always a good stress and anxiety reducer to have a couple of small crystals in your pocket as an emotional intelligence anchor. I used this strategy every time I would speak in front of large audiences and when I was paired with a partner on presentations, I always gave that person one or two to carry as well. This gesture resonates very strongly with people. Years later I still receive picture messages from leaders who are holding crystals that they'll put in their pockets before going onstage to present. You can tie appreciation anchors into your company's vision and/or mission for a great tangible item that will remind your employees of your culture.

Other great appreciation anchors include stress-reducing pamphlets, books, or daily affirmation calendars that have quotes/tips for relaxation or instructions on how to breathe and center oneself. (See my "Resources" page.)

POSITIVE AFFIRMATION CARDS

Put together a bowl containing cards with inspirational affirmations or quotes listed on each one. Packs of these are available online, or see my "Resources" page. At the end of your meeting or session, have each person close their eyes and take a deep, centering breath. Have them reach into the bowl with their eyes closed and pull out a life affirmation quote that is meant just for them. If they would like, they can read the message they received to their peers and share their thoughts. Let them keep the card as a reminder of the message they received. This is such a quick, influential way to end a meeting and leave everyone with a positive, inspired mindset. People seem to just get what was meant for them, and I am contacted years later with pictures from individuals who still have their cards.

EXPRESSIONS OF GRATITUDE

Grateful people sleep better. Gratitude improves self-esteem. Gratitude enhances empathy and reduces aggression.

—"7 SCIENTIFICALLY PROVEN BENEFITS OF GRATITUDE THAT WILL MOTIVATE YOU TO GIVE THANKS YEAR-ROUND," AMY MORIN, FORBES

A great way to kick off a meeting with a group or an individual is to start by sharing what they are

grateful for. Start your sessions off with each individual reporting on what they are grateful for that day, week, or month. They can choose something related to business or their personal life to help create a connection with the overall group.

MEETING ENVIRONMENTS

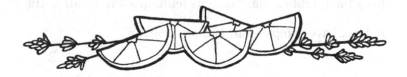

For in-person meetings, make sure you arrive early to set up the room. Bring an essential oil diffuser, and put some lavender, which raises positive vibrations, or a balancing blend into it. This will set the tone in the room. Make sure that you have snacks and drinks readily available as well. If individuals are stressed out or hungry, their brains may not be open to creativity and possibility. The goal is to make your employees as comfortable as possible, so their creativity and inspiration can shine through in the meeting.

WITH GRATITUDE

I am hoping that after reading about all these activities and modalities your creativity is flowing, and you try each one in your own way. Whether it is with a group of people, coworkers, a clients, friends, or family members, these activities can be translated throughout all parts of your life to help foster human connection and bring back into our lives the qualities that make us human, such as our ability to love, have compassion, and be creative.

When I was born into this world

The only things I knew were to love,

laugh, and shine my light brightly.

Then as I grew, people told me to stop

laughing. "Take life seriously," they said,

"If you want to get ahead in this

world." So I stopped laughing.

People told me, "Be careful who you love If

you don't want your heart broken."

So I stopped loving.

They said, "Don't shine your light so bright As

it draws too much attention onto you."

So I stopped shining And became small And withered

And died

Only to learn upon death That all that matters in life

Is to love, laugh, and shine our light brightly!

—ANITA MOORJANI

RESOURCES

For all downloadable activities listed in the book,
please visit www.createmagicatwork.net.

Pamphlet: *How to Relax,* by Thich Nhat Hanh.

Journals and Journal Prompt Cards: www.
createmagicatwork.net.

Question Prompt Cards: "What's Your Word?"
MyIntent.org.

Recommended essential oils: doterra, lavender,
elevation, and/or motivation.

Flying Wish Paper: Amazon.

Affirmation/Inspirational Cards: "Power Thought
Cards," by Lousie Hay; "I Can Do It" cards, by
Louise Hay.

Daily Affirmation Calendar: "I Can Do It," by
Louise Hay.

Tea Mugs: www.createmagicatwork.net.

Printed in the United States
by Baker & Taylor Publisher Services

Printed in the United States
by Baker & Taylor Publisher Services